Surrey Buses
In Camera

by David Kaye

QUOTES LIMITED of BUCKINGHAM

MCMXCII

Published by Quotes Limited
Buckingham, England

Typeset in Plantin by
Key Composition, Northampton, England

Pictures Lithographed by
South Midlands Lithoplates Limited, Luton, England

Printed by Busiprint Limited
Buckingham, England

Bound by Charles Letts Limited
Edinburgh, Scotland

© David Kaye 1992

ISBN 0 86023 393 6

Acknowledgements

The author is grateful for all the help he has received from so many people in the compilation of this collection, and would like to thank especially Mr D. W. K. Jones and Mr J. C. Sutton, without whose assistance this project would never have come to fruition.

Surrey has long been dominated in the west by Aldershot & District/Alder Valley and London Transport in the east, so that photographs of these operators fill many pages. Nevertheless there has been always a sprinkling of small independent operators, and this has been especially true of the Guildford-Woking area. These, too, have been covered. Tillingbourne Valley has for the past 67 years been one of them. During the Second World War someone wrote a poem about them entitled *An Appreciation of the 8.13*. One verse ran as follows:

'Faithful Tilly! Big or little,
Steered by Jack or Bert to town,
Red and grey bus, crammed with people,
Over lovely Merrow Down.'

Throughout this book the pre-1974 boundaries of Surrey have been observed.

The volume is dedicated to my cousin, the novelist Sarah Shears, herself a resident of Merrow. Without her enthusiasm and encouragement over the past thirty years, this author would never have gone into print.

AFD	Anthony F. Drewitt	JCB	J.C. Bates
AVPL	A.V.P. LaCroix	JFH	J.F. Higham
CAH	Charles A. Hibbert	JSC	John Sutton Collection
CCC	Coral C. Combs	KH	Kingston upon Thames Heritage
CRM	Crown Royal Mail		
CJW	W.J. Wigley	LTB	London Transport Board
DK	David Kaye	NH	N. Hamshere
DWKJ	D.W.K. Jones	NHC	N. Hamshere Collection
EC	Epsom Coaches	NVM	N.V. Martin
GAR	Geoff A. Rixon	RL	Richmond upon Thames Library
GBE	G.B. Elliott		
HJS	H.J. Snook	RHGS	R.H.G. Simpson
	SC	Safeguard Collection	

3

Surrey in the 1990s is commuter territory, scythed through by the M3 and M25. One hundred and fifty years ago it had few large towns and generally poor public transport. In 1836 five Royal Mail coaches crossed the county to Brighton (*via* Reigate), Falmouth and Penzance (*via* Bagshot), Poole (*via* Farnham) and Portsmouth (*via* Kingston upon Thames). There were also stage coaches passing through to the south coast, especially serving Kingston upon Thames (16), Guildford (15), and Bagshot, Camberley and Redhill (12 each). However, by 1851 *The Illustrated Omnibus Guide* lists only three such coaches, for by then the railway had arrived, creating new towns such as Woking.

On 17 April 1883 the first horse trams arrived in the county, when the West Metropolitan Tramways Company opened a line between Kew Bridge and Lower Mortlake Road, Richmond upon Thames. Later, on 1 March 1906, the London United Tramways electric cars began operating between Surbiton and Kingston upon Thames, with branch lines to Dittons and Tolworth. Later that year other lines oened to Ham Common and Richmond Park Gates, while in 1907 a further extension joined Kingston upon Thames with Wimbledon. However, the Kew - Richmond horse tramway was not electrified and it closed down on 20 April 1912. Meanwhile LCC tram routes 2 and 4 crossed the Surrey border into Wimbledon.

On the western side of the county the Aldershot & Farnborough Motor Omnibus Company was founded on 11 May 1906, becoming the Aldershot & District Traction Company in July 1912, with five routes out of Aldershot to Ash Vale, Deepcut Camps, Farnborough, Farnham and Fleet. Gradually they bought up other operators such as Guildford & District Motor Services soon after the end of the First World War. This brought them into physical contact with Dennis Bros, who were to supply them with 'buses and coaches in large numbers, so that by 1927 nearly all the fleet of 158 vehicles was of that make.

In the Guildford area A&D had competition from newer, but smaller operators, such as Arthur Newman's Safeguard Coaches (formed in 1924), G. Trice's Tillingbourne Valley (1924) and S. Hayter's Yellow Bus Service (1921). In addition there were Lock's Blue Saloon (which ran out of Woking), George Redding's Magnet (to Shelford) B. Hammond & Sons, and G. Waller's Gastonia Coaches (of Cranleigh). In the north of the county J. P. Fox traded as Woking & District, operating out to Camberley and Staines. Like so many other such independents, Woking & District was acquired by Aldershot & District, in 1930.

In the east of the county the first horse 'bus route appears c1896, run by A. W. Wickens at weekends between Reigate and Redhill, replacing his vehicle on 16 October 1905 with a secondhand 40hp motorbus. In Dorking Mr Fairbrother, who kept the Windmill public house, ran a horse 'bus, as did Mr Hensman, whose service was based at the Holly and Laurel at Holmwood, some three miles out of Dorking on the Horsham road.

However, the formation of the East Surrey Traction Company by Arthur Henry Hawkins on 23 May 1911 brought about the true motorbus era on this side of the county. Their first route was between Reigate and Redhill. By May 1914 ESTC was also operating to Dorking, Godstone, Holmwood, Horley, Merstham and Westerham, using Daimlers and Leylands. However, the London General Omnubis Company began popular summer Sunday excursions to Dorking, Leatherhead and Reigate, their delights outlined in the free booklet *The Heart of Surrey*. So in 1921 an agreement was reached between the LGOC and ESTCo, whereby they split up their rural services south of Croydon, using the new AEC 'K' class of open-top double-deckers, necessitating the following admonition:

'Passengers travelling on top of the bus are warned to keep their seats while the vehicle is in motion, and to beware of railway bridges, overhanging trees, telegraph wires, etc.'

The 1920s saw the establishment of a network of express and limited stop routes between Surrey and Central London. In 1926 A&D began such a service from Farnham. That year Charles Dobbs started his Skylark Motor Coach Company's hourly service between Guildford and Oxford Circus, *via* Esher and the new Kingston by-pass. In 1930 London General commenced their new Green Line network with such routes as: C (Chertsey-London), D (Dorking-London), G (Guildford-London), H (Harpenden-Great Bookham), K (Caterham-Hemel Hempstead), R (Reigate-London) and T (Tring-Godstone).

On 1 July 1933 the London Passenger Transport Board came into effect, and this meant not only the absorption of East Surrey Traction, but the curtailment of Aldershot & District routes to the western half of the county. Among the trams taken over by the LPTB were 52 cars of the South Metropolitan Electric Tramways and 55 of Croydon Corporation. Incidentally, Croydon had been the scene of late 19th century experiments with battery, compressed air and even naphtha-powered trams!

On 15 June 1931 London United Tramways had substituted AEC 663T trolleybuses (nicknamed 'Diddlers') on three of their tram routes, bringing into operation trolleybus routes 1 (Kingston-Twickenham), 3 (Kingston Hill-Tolworth) and 4 (Wimbledon-Hampton Court). In July route 2 (Kingston Hill-Dittons) commenced. Elsewhere, on 12 May 1937 trams were ousted by trolleybuses on new route 630 (Scrubs Lane-West Croydon), establishing the only trolleybus depôt in Surrey at Sutton (renamed Carshalton in 1950), with a complement of 51 vehicles.

Seaside excursions became increasingly popular in the 1930s, being operated by specialist firms like Bourne & Balmer (Croydon), Epsom Coaches and Surrey Motors, while smaller businesses such as Pearl Grey (who used to tout for trade in Guildford's North Street), and Cooke's Coaches (also of Guildford) joined in this profitable trade.

Throughout Britain services were restricted during the Second World War. Both the LPTB and A&D took delivery of 'utility' double-deckers, while a few of the equally austere Bedford OWB single-deckers entered service with small operators, eg: Tillingbourne Valley.

In the immediate post-war boom in public transport some new coach firms started up, such as Mr A. Pullen's Banstead Coaches in 1959. A 1948 list of independent Surrey stage carriage operators revealed nine (five of them in the Guildford area). Basil Williams's ephemeral Hants & Sussex empire moved into the south of the county with the acquisition of F. H. Kilner (Transport) of Loxwood, but all were withdrawn in 1954 following bankruptcy proceedings. A&D bought out Hammond & Sons of Wonersh in 1953 and Yellow Bus Services in 1958. However, deregulation in 1986 has brought about a rebirth of the small operator, such as a relaunch of Blue Saloon in Guildford.

Green Line services were suspended as from September 1942, and not restarted until 1946, when routes 706-718 crossed the county. In May 1951 the new underfloor-engined AEC 'Regal IV's' modernised these operations, and in 1960 double-deck 'Routemasters' began to appear on some Surrey limited-stop routes.

Aldershot & District continued to patronise Dennis Bros until they ceased to manufacture 'buses and, although this side was restarted in the 1980s, they have not found favour with local operators, although appearing in many fleets in the East Midlands. On 1 January 1969 A&D became part of the new National Bus Company, with its policy of buying Bristol and Leyland vehicles. In 1972 A&D was merged with another NBC constituent, Thames Valley Traction, the new operator being known as Alder Valley, the fleet repainted poppy red and white. London Country Bus Services also became part of NBC, and since privatisation have become London & Country.

A garden seat horse 'bus in Church Street, Reigate at the turn of the century. (HJS)

Originally built by G. H. Goldby of Fulham in 1880, this horse 'bus operated between Dorking and Holmwood. Then, in 1973, it was rescued in a decayed condition by Tony Drewitt, who rebuilt it to celebrate the 150th anniversary of Shillibeer's first London omnibus in 1979. Here it is seen running again in Dorking that year. (AFD)

The first tramway laid down in the county was this one between the Surrey side of Kew Bridge and Richmond upon Thames. It remained horse-drawn until its closure in 1912. (RL)

Seen at Kingston upon Thames, London United Tramways car 233 was a type 'W', built by the British Electric Car Company on Brill 22E maximum traction trucks in 1902. Although some of this class were given canopy roofs at a later date this tram remained open-top, running on routes to Dittons (73), Hampton Court (71), Richmond (69), Tolworth (77) and Wimbledon (71). (KH)

P 7228 was one of the first 'buses purchased by East Surrey Traction Company, and was a Leyland with a Liversidge body. Here it is seen working the main road route between Redhill and Reigate in the heartland of East Surrey territory. (HJS)

East Surrey's No 20 (PA 9575) was an AEC double-decker, originally built for London General. This 34-seater is on route S22, which ran along the eastern extremity of Surrey into Sussex at East Grinstead. (HJS)

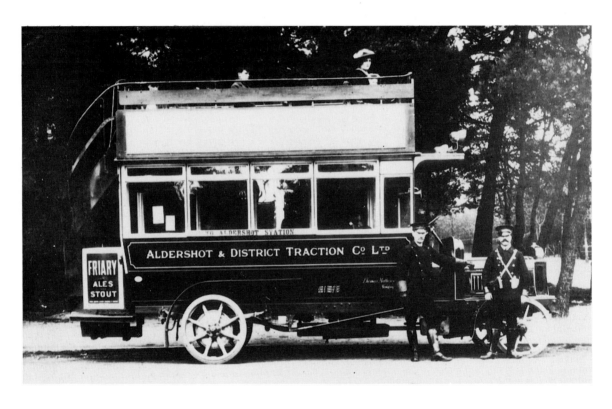

On the opposite fringe of the county, Aldershot & District were crossing the Hampshire border into Farnham. Unlike the East Surrey double-decker, it lacks safety guard-rails under its high chassis. (JSC)

FRONT COVER: A single-decker Daimler CB of the same period, also in the early fleet of A&D, on service to Guildford. Its registration (AB 3342) suggests that it may have been a secondhand vehicle. Note the unusually mounted headlamps. (TES)

At Cranleigh, where a former brewery had been converted into Frank Osbourn's workshops, there stand these three period vehicles. On the left is LC 5309, a typical Edwardian, small, enclosed 'bus. On the right is PA 5051, a small Ford Model 'T' charabanc of the type that many small operators equipped themselves with after the First World War. Between them is P 5879, with its impressive array of lamps. (CCC)

Epsom Coaches also ran a Model 'T' chara, in this case seating fourteen, although this photograph shows fifteen on board! (EC)

This Model 'T' was for stage carriage work with Royal Blue, operated by F. W. Kerridge of Milford on his network of routes from Godalming to Dunsfold and to Hambledon; c1927 it was replaced by a Bean. (GBE)

One of the small operators in the Guildford area was Magnet, who ran this little Chevrolet on the picturesque route out to Peaslake via Newlands Corner, the Silent Pool and Shere. (HJS)

It is May 1926 and in Reigate the driver of this Graves charabanc is touting for trade to beat the transport workers, who were supporting the General Strike. The return fare to London on this fascinating little vehicle is being advertised as six shillings. (HJS)

An East Surrey inspector awaits the departure of No 77 (PE 1417), an AEC 2-tonner from Reigate Town Hall for Redhill, via Blackborough Road. (HJS)

East Surrey also operated double-deckers of AEC manufacture, as this AEC NS demonstrates. No PS 1758 (PE 9180) is seen in its latter days when finishing its life in the ranks of London Transport. Later 'buses of this class had enclosed roofs. (DWKJ)

London General Country Tilling-Stevens B10A, PG 9381 is on route 36 (later 436) between Guildford and Staines, via Woking. (JFH)

PH 3314, a London General Country Services ADC, is seen here at the end of its active life in February 1936. (DWKJ)

Built in 1928, PH 1205 was an AEC 419, belonging to East Surrey Traction, and is seen here on Reigate Heath near the wooden postmill. Called an 'all weather' coach, its canvas roof has been folded back. Note the doors at both the front and rear of the vehicle. (HJS)

Some small Chevrolet LO models had their chassis extended to become six wheelers in the late 1920s. Here is one such example (PH 4809), owned by Safeguard Bus Services of Guildford. (SC)

PK 4244 was one of the last open-top double-decker Tilling-Stevens to be delivered to East Surrey. It was later sold for further service to Canvey Transport, with whom it is depicted in 1937. (DWKJ)

By 1930 covered-top double-deckers had become increasingly common, such as Aldershot & District D263 (OU 1112), a Dennis 'H' with a Hall & Lewis body. Here it is on a local route to Guildford Park. (DWKJ)

In March 1936, this line-up of withdrawn London Transport double-deckers stood at Guildford, including GU 977 and VX 1361, two locally-built Dennis 'Hs'. (DWKJ)

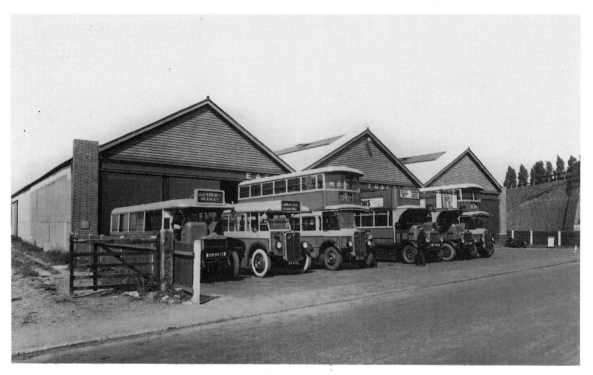

A fascinating 1930 line-up of AECs outside the East Surrey Traction garage at Leatherhead (opened in 1925 and still in operation); from left to right: XW 9877 (a 'K'), PG 678 ('Regal'), PG 7726 ('Regent'), PF 9020 ('PS'), PC 9317 ('S') and PG 7xx ('Regent'). The 'PS' class was the ESTC version of London General's 'NS' class. (CJW)

London General's AEC 'Regal' T1 (UU 6616) of 1929 had a 30-seater body constructed by the operator. Four years later it entered the ranks of the newly established London Passenger Transport Board. It is seen on route 216 between Kingston upon Thames and Staines (where it stands), via Sunbury. (DWKJ.)

The Green Line version of the 'T' class (like T223, GK 5491) had mounted roof boards. This one is on a limited-stop route R from Hitchin to Reigate, via Oxford Circus and Sutton. (AVPL)

One of the private operators taken over by the LPTB for Green Line services was Skylark of High Wycombe, who patronised their local coach-assembler, Gilford. This particular route ran between London and Guildford, via Esher and Chobham. (JFH)

The Reigate overhaul works with various operators' coaches, including a Skylark Gilford (MT 1954), the second vehicle from the left. (HJS)

KX 7164 was a smaller Gilford AS6, acquired by the LPTB. By March 1935 it had been demoted to working stage carriage services like route 462 into Leatherhead. (DWKJ)

Another acquisition for Green Line was PL 6459, a Morris Commercial 'Viceroy', demonstrating the amazing variety of types to be found in its ranks in the early 1930s. (HJS)

Among the smallest of such purchases was BD23 (PJ 8430), a 20-seater Bedford WLB of 1932. At one time operated by Sunshine Coaches, it was photographed along the Victoria Embankment in 1935. (DWKJ)

Aldershot & District also ran small vehicles like this Morris Commercial No M1 (CG 755), which worked a service that crossed the Hampshire border into Petersfield. (JFH).

T396 (PG 7839) started life as an AEC 'Regal' with East Surrey Traction before being transferred into London Transport's country fleet. In 1938 this distinctive body was replaced by a more orthodox LPTB one. (DWKJ)

The well-known Croydon coach operator, Bourne & Balmer, ran an excursion fleet to the seaside before the Second World War with vehicles like No 25 (OY 3291), a Dennis 'Arrow'. (NVM)

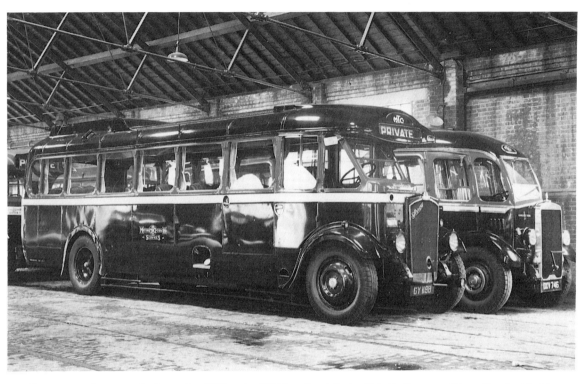

Seen nearest the camera in September 1937 at the Old Kent Road depôt of M. T. Company (Motor Coaches) Ltd is another Dennis 'Arrow', GY 1198 of 1932, with its 32-seat London Lorries body. In 1938 it was purchased by Safeguard of Guildford, who only used it for two years. (DWKJ)

Kingston upon Thames Bus Station is the background for one of London Transport's red AEC 'Q' side-engined 'buses of 1935 (Q21, BXD 542) and green T469 (ELP 193) of 1938, operating 'red' route 218 to Staines. (DWKJ).

Built in 1934, this LPTB Dennis 'Ace' stands outside the Horse and Groom in Guildford (scene years later of a bomb outrage) on service 448 to Peaslake. (JFH)

The Walton-on-Thames Motor Company operated a short route between the railway station and their garage near Walton Bridge, using CPF 349, also a Dennis 'Ace' (known affectionately as 'Flying Pigs'). When this shot was taken in 1937, the 'bus was two years old. (DWKJ)

Much rarer was the Dennis 'Pike'. This one also had a Dennis body. GPF 117 belonged to the Yellow Bus Services of Guildford and is seen here emerging from a typical Surrey sunken lane en route between its home town and Farnham. It was built in 1938. (NHC)

London Transport Country ST 1139 (UU 6610) dated from 1929, and was working out of East Grinstead garage on route 409 to West Croydon, via Lingfield and Coulsdon Common in September 1938, when this view was taken. (DWKJ)

The batch of a dozen London Transport Country AEC 'Regents' STL 1044-55 were always known by enthusiasts as the 'Godstone STLs', as they spent the bulk of their working lives based at that garage. Unlike the rest of their class, they had Weymann lowbridge bodies. Here STL 1054 (BPF 457) is on route 410 to Bromley over the Kent border, via Godstone and Westerham, in the immediate post-war period. (DWKJ)

In contrast STL 2417 (EGO 470) of 1938 has a more orthodox highbridge body as it waits to depart from Godstone garage for Caterham in 1940. Note the eye-catching Picture Post *advertisements on either side of the destination box.*
(DWKJ)

Prior to the Second World War Aldershot & District built up a handsome fleet of Strachan-bodied Dennis 'Lancets' for express work and for seaside excursions. Here No 492 (BOT 288) poses with its extensive roof luggage rack. (JSC)

ABOVE: *Immediately before the outbreak of hostilities in 1939, London Transport introduced their CR class of rear-engined Leyland 'Cubs' — very much ahead of their time. Here CR43 (FXT 149) is on local Epsom route 481 in 1953. (GAR) OPPOSITE: The experimental fully-fronted London Transport STL 857 (BXD 582) of 1934 was also in advance of general designs of that period. This posed shot was taken in November 1935 with its blinds turned to route 73A to Richmond. (LTB)*

49

Another attempt at streamlining came after the Second World War with the arrival on the Green Line 711 route (High Wycombe to Reigate) of RTC1 (FXT 272). This started life as an ordinary RT97, an AEC 'Regent', in 1940, but its body was destroyed by enemy action in July 1944. At first it was rebuilt as a pay-as-you-enter bus, but was rebuilt again as a double-decker coach in 1949.

Working a 1953 Derby Day special from Morden Station to Epsom Race Course is London Transport D44 (GXV 775), a Daimler CWA6 with a Brush 'utility' body. It is followed by RT 2357 (KGU 386) with its front top deck windows half-lowered. (GAR)

Aldershot & District also took delivery of wartime 'buses, including No 888 (EOT 25), a Guy 'Arab II'. Its 'utility'
body, as seen here, was replaced by a new East Lancs one in 1954. (JFH)

*Waiting to depart on the local Guildford route to Warren Road is Tillingbourne Valley Bedford OB. MNU 689 had
a rare Woodall Nicholson 29-seat body. This vehicle was bought secondhand in 1951 and resold in 1960. (DK)*

LEFT: Another Tillingbourne Valley vehicle was MPE 296, an Austin CXB of 1948 with a Plaxton 29-seat body, also bound for Warren Road. (DK) RIGHT: Brown Motor Services (operated by Brady of Forest Green) OPB 536 was a much rarer Leyland 'Comet' of 1950 with a Duple body, about to depart on the daily service to Ewhurst. (DK)

An unusual full-fronted version of the Bedford OB is seen here in JTB 262 with its Plaxton body, working on Hammond's route out of Guildford. (DK)

Yet another view of a Bedford OB, this time with the popular Duple body. HOT 339 had started its working life in the expanding fleet of Hants & Sussex but, when this view was taken of it at Horsham's Carfax, it was operated by Brown Motor Services on their route out to Holmbury St Mary. (DK)

Bourne & Balmer's Dennis 'Lancet' No 41 (ORK 441) had a half-cab Harrington body, and is seen here on hire to London Transport, opeating their route 133 (South Croydon - Liverpool Street). (DWKJ)

OPPOSITE: The cover of a Yellow Bus Services timetable, featuring PPA 649, a 1951 Dennis 'Lancet' J10, with a partially full-fronted Gurney Nutting 39-seat coach body on the route from Guildford to Farnham. (JSC)
ABOVE: In 1953 Aldershot & District ordered this one-off underfloor- engined version of the Dennis 'Lancet' with a Strachan body. No 187 (KOR 600) passed through the hands of Reliance of Grantham, before working into Windsor with Blue Bus of Slough in 1963. (DK)

These two interesting saloons began life with Yellow Bus Services, but both ended it with Chiltern Queens of Woodcote, Berkshire. SPD 207 was a 1952 Dennis 'Falcon' P5 with a 30-seat Gurney Nutting body, while 530 BPG was the unique 1956 underfloor-engined Dennis 'Pelican', with its 44-seat Duple (Midland) 'bus body. (JCB)

Aldershot & District No 223 (LOU 51) was a 1954 Dennis 'Lance' K4 powered by a Gardner 5LW engine and fitted with a 56-seat Weymann lowbridge body. It awaits departure at Guildford on route 67 to nearby Wood Street. (DK)

The replacement for the 'Lance' in the fleet of Aldershot & District was the Dennis 'Loline', a version of the successful Bristol 'Lodekka' built under licence. This demonstration vehicle is in the Earls Court 'bus and coach park at a Commercial Motor Show. (DK)

Aldershot & District No 501 (501 KOT) was a Dennis 'Loline III' with a Weymann 68-seat body built in 1964. It is viewed here at Guildford. Over its front entrance was a small 'via' blind, which on local routes often showed the confusing information 'TO & FROM'! (DK)

Single-deckers were ousted by green London Transport RLHs, based on AEC 'Regent III' chassis and with 53-seat Weymann lowbridge bodywork on the routes in North-west Surrey that had to cope with the Woking railway underpass. Here RLH 27 (MXX 227) of 1952 stands outside the Library at Walton-on-Thames on route 461A to St Peter's Hospital at Botleys Park. (DK)

LEFT: In another part of Walton-on-Thames, highbridge AEC 'Regent' RT 4077 (LUC 426) is at the terminus of route 131 to Kingston-upon-Thames, via the Moleseys. (DK) RIGHT: A 1952 AEC 'Regal IV' with a 41-seat Metro-Cammell all-metal body, RF496 (MXX 473) picks up members of a local transport club in 1960 on route 218 from Staines to Kingston upon Thames. (DK)

Although most of them had served elsewhere than Surrey in their London Transport days, a dozen of these Guy 'Vixen' Specials, with their 26-seat ECW bodies, ended up in the ranks of Tillingbourne Valley. In this photograph, ex-GS84 (MXX 384) stands at Guildford waiting to depart to Peaslake. (DK)

Aldershot & District Nos 173 & 183 (HOU 899/909) were 1950 vintage Dennis 'Lancet' J10s with 38-seat rear-entrance Strachan bodies, the last such combination of manufacturers to enter the fleet. (NH)

London Transport's Q1 class of trolleybuses replaced the AEC 663T 'Diddlers' in the Kingston upon Thames area in 1948. 1779 (HYM 779) was a BUT 9641T with an MCW 77-seat body. It is seen in Wimbledon when two years old. (GAR)

The sad scene at London Transport's Fulwell garage on 13 June 1962, shortly after the final trolleybus closure; the vehicles nearest the camera are members of class L1, AEC-MCW chassisless trolleybuses. (CAH)

LEFT: Whiteley Village was built by the philanthropic founder of that famous London department store for his retired staff, and was near Walton-on-Thames. The two places were linked by this free 'bus service, operated in the late 1950s by WPB 154, a Thames 'bus. (DK) RIGHT: Walton-on-Thames Motor Company purchased this Bedford OB with its Mulliner 28-seat body from Silvey of Epney, Gloucestershire, in June 1954. JDF 306 is waiting to pick up passengers at the railway station. (DK)

Safeguard changed from purchasing Dennises to buying Bedfords in 1954. 699 VPL is an SB model with a 41-seat Duple (Midland) body, here leaving Guildford Cathedral on Stag Hill, after the Dennisville route had been extended there in 1963. (DK)

Safeguard changed again to the AEC 'Reliance' in 1962 for their stage carriage fleet. Two years later they took into stock EPB 189 B, with its handsome 53-seat Willowbrook body, here departing from the centre of Guildford to Westborough. (DK)

Still going strong in 1972 was PPF 492, a Harrington-bodied coach belonging to Surrey Motors, who specialised in excursion work, often to south coast resorts. (JSC)

RPE 823, the 'Surrey Queen', was in the fleet of Rackcliffe, who also ran Cooke's Coaches of Guildford. In this shot it is taking part in a carnival procession with the theme 'Our Heritage: the Sea - Transport Elizabeth I & II', and is surmounted by a model of a Tudor ship. (NH)

Thames Valley Traction Bristol MW6G of 1960, with its dual-purpose 41-seat ECW body, loads up at Guildford for the long joint route 75 with Aldershot & District to Reading in 1965. (DK)

Aldershot & District no 268 (MOR 599) was an AEC 'Reliance' of 1954 with a 41-seat central-entrance Strachan coach body, and was used principally on the Farnham to London expresss service. (RHGS)

The express duties were taken over in 1962 by newer 'Reliances' with Park Royal 49-seat front-entrance coach bodies, like No 469 (469 FCG). (RHGS)

The first Surrey Post Office 'bus service started on 2 August 1973 between Ockley and Dorking, followed by Oxted-Lingfield on 24 September. Later came Reigate-Leigh and Redhill-Outwood. This view shows the first one near Coldharbour on Dorking Common. (CRM)

Tailpiece: Guildford's North Street in August 1991 with a London Country Leyland National Series 2 on the long-established route 436. Many of this operator's single-deckers nowadays are minibuses, however. (DK)

Index to Illustrations